Copyright © 2024 by Jamie Greenwood/Monique Meerseman

All rights reserved. No part of this book or its illustrations may be reproduced, copied, or reused in any form or by any means, electronic or mechanical, without the prior written permission of the author, Jamie Greenwood, or the illustrator, Monique Meerseman. Unauthorized use or reproduction of the contents or illustrations is prohibited and may be subject to legal action. For inquiries, please contact the author or illustrator for written consent.

TO THE CHILDREN OF SONSHINE COMMUNITY SCHOOL IN MINAMBA ZAMBIA

in recognition of their endeavours to want an education for a better tomorrow.

Many children use to walk 20 km to school and some still do. Today because of GTM Zambian Sonshine and their donors, children are able to receive an education in their local community.

Profits from this book will be going to continue educational efforts in Zambia. For more information go to gtmzambiansonshine.com.

In a land so distant, a tale takes flight,
A rabbit, quite sad, in the bright, warming light.
He scrubbed his ears, paws licked with delight,
To be the cleanest, he'd toil day and night.
But folks all around, they'd yell in a fuss,
"Unclean, unclean!"
They'd flee, leave him without trust.
This bunny, perplexed, tried hard, never quit,
To win back their hearts, though they'd label him unfit.

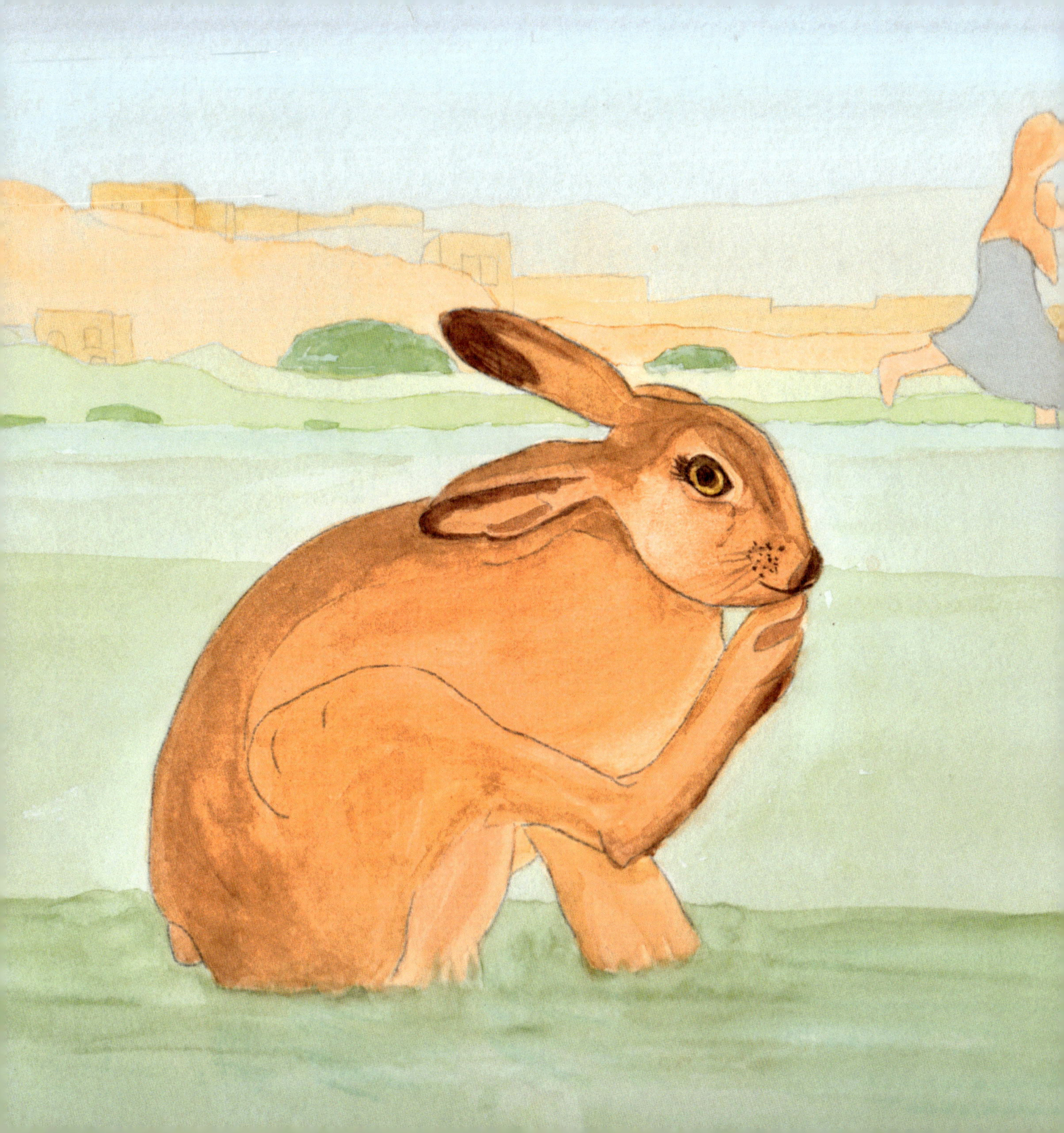

Now, one fine day, dear Easter, so shy,
Hid in the bushes, oh my, oh my!
Yearned to join folks, but oh, so discreet,
"Unclean, unclean!" made his heart skip a beat.
So there he stayed, hidden, quiet and hushed,
In the thicket, he peeked, oh, he mushed and he mushed.
Watching a blind beggar, with tender, kind grace,
A tale of compassion in this peculiar place.

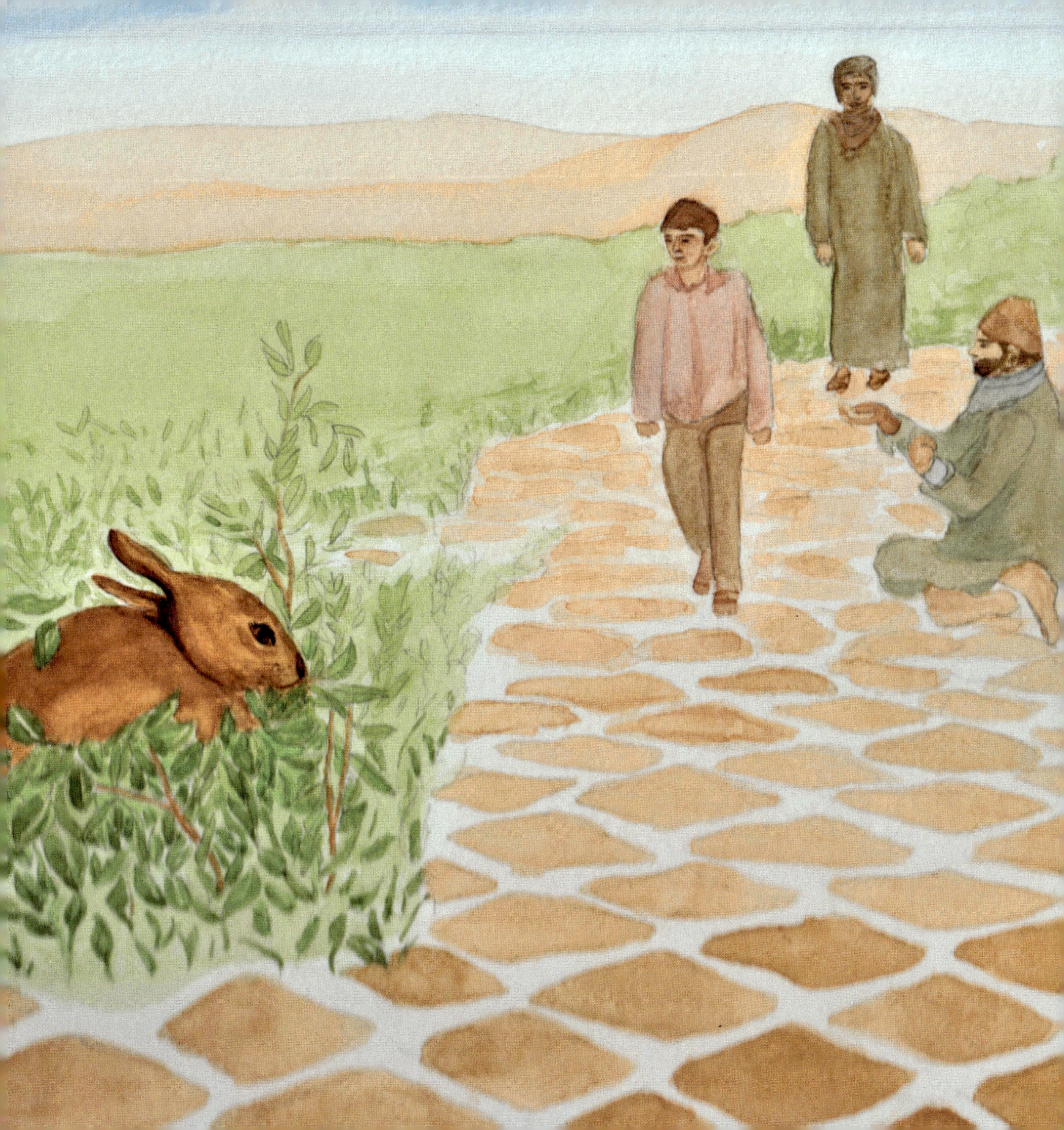

The blind beggar, ignored by many, the rabbit did relate,
Sitting quietly, he'd commiserate.
But one fine day, a stranger drew near,
Spit and mud magic, to the rabbit's ear unclear.
The beggar sprang up, dashed to a pond so bright,
Miraculously seeing, he vanished from sight.
As if blindness had fled, like a fleeting dream,
In a moment, he dashed, no longer unseen.

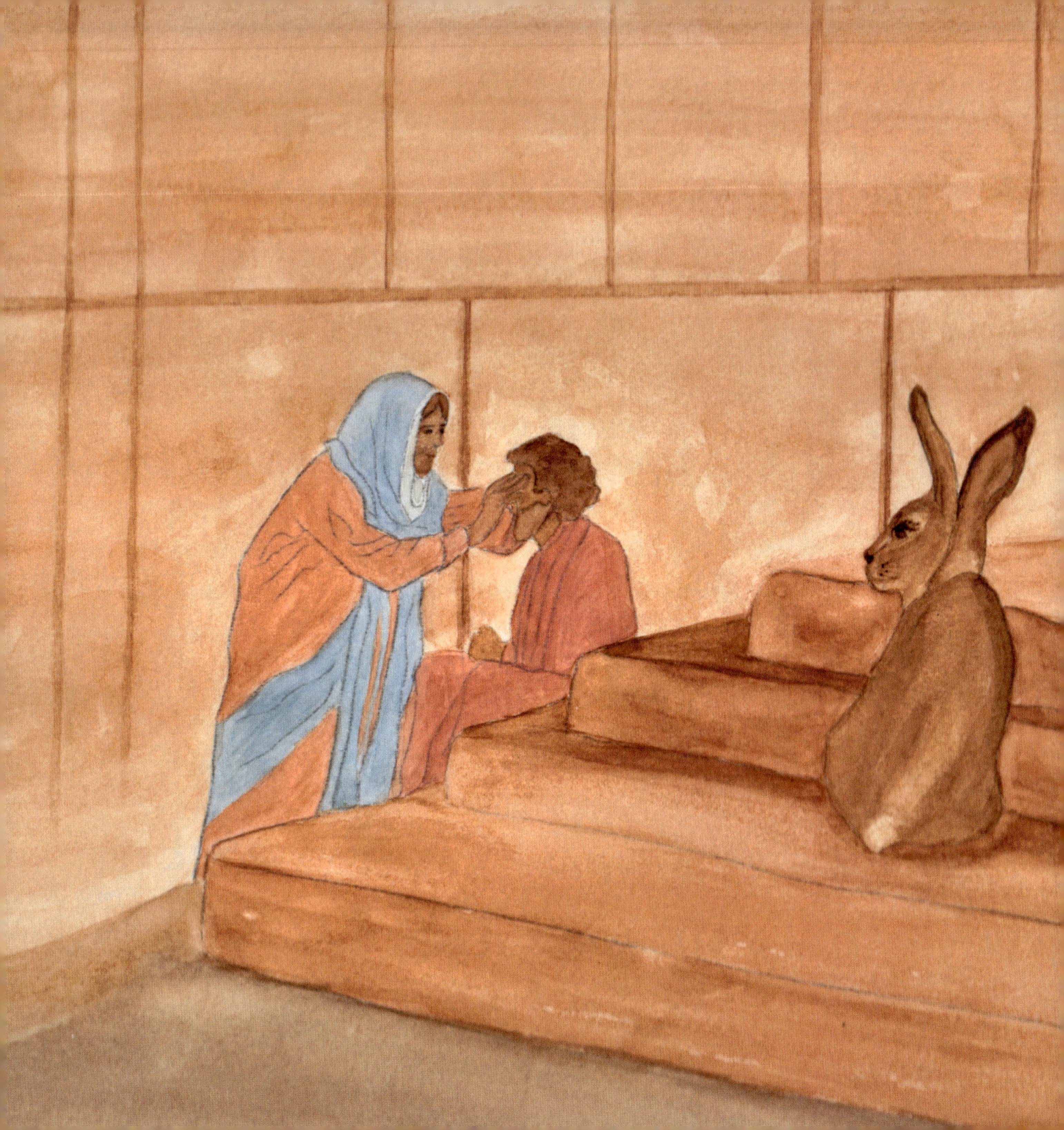

Easter trailed the man, so cautious, so keen,
From the shadows, he watched, oh, quite unseen.
With curiosity bound, but always at bay,
Never near enough, for clean he could never sway.
From afar he observed, in the moonlight's soft gleam,
The man's scent was a puzzle, like a faraway dream.
Dust and dirt in the mix, and a scent so supreme,
Easter sniffed the air, a hint of perfume it would seem.

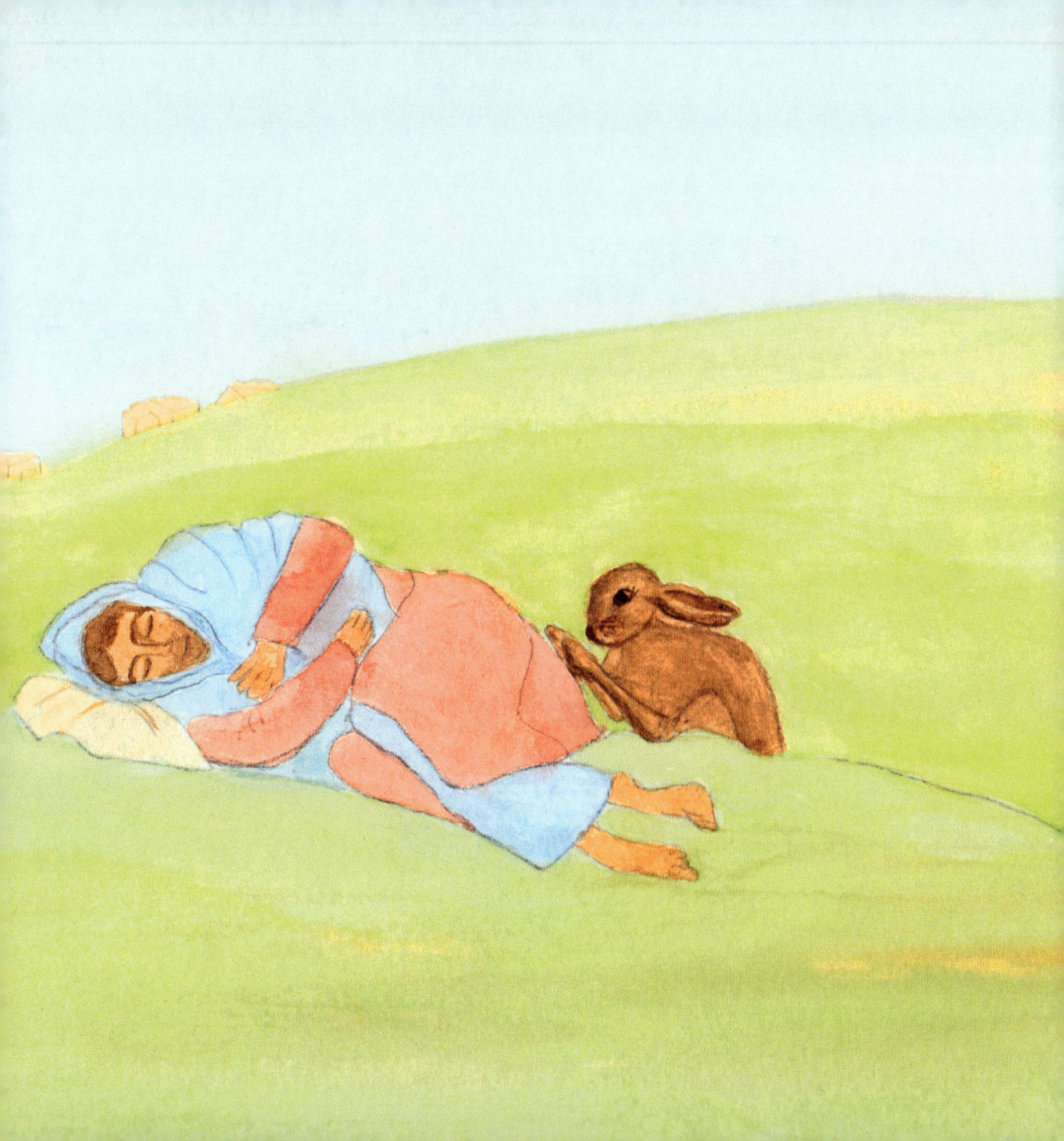

Perfume's sweet aroma, Easter's nose did meet
As he nestled at the man's feet, so discreet.
He thought he'd rest a bit, with heart's rapid beat,
In dread that awoke, the cry "Unclean" would repeat.
Pondering the scent, he drifted to slumber so deep,
In the gentle embrace of this mysterious sleep.

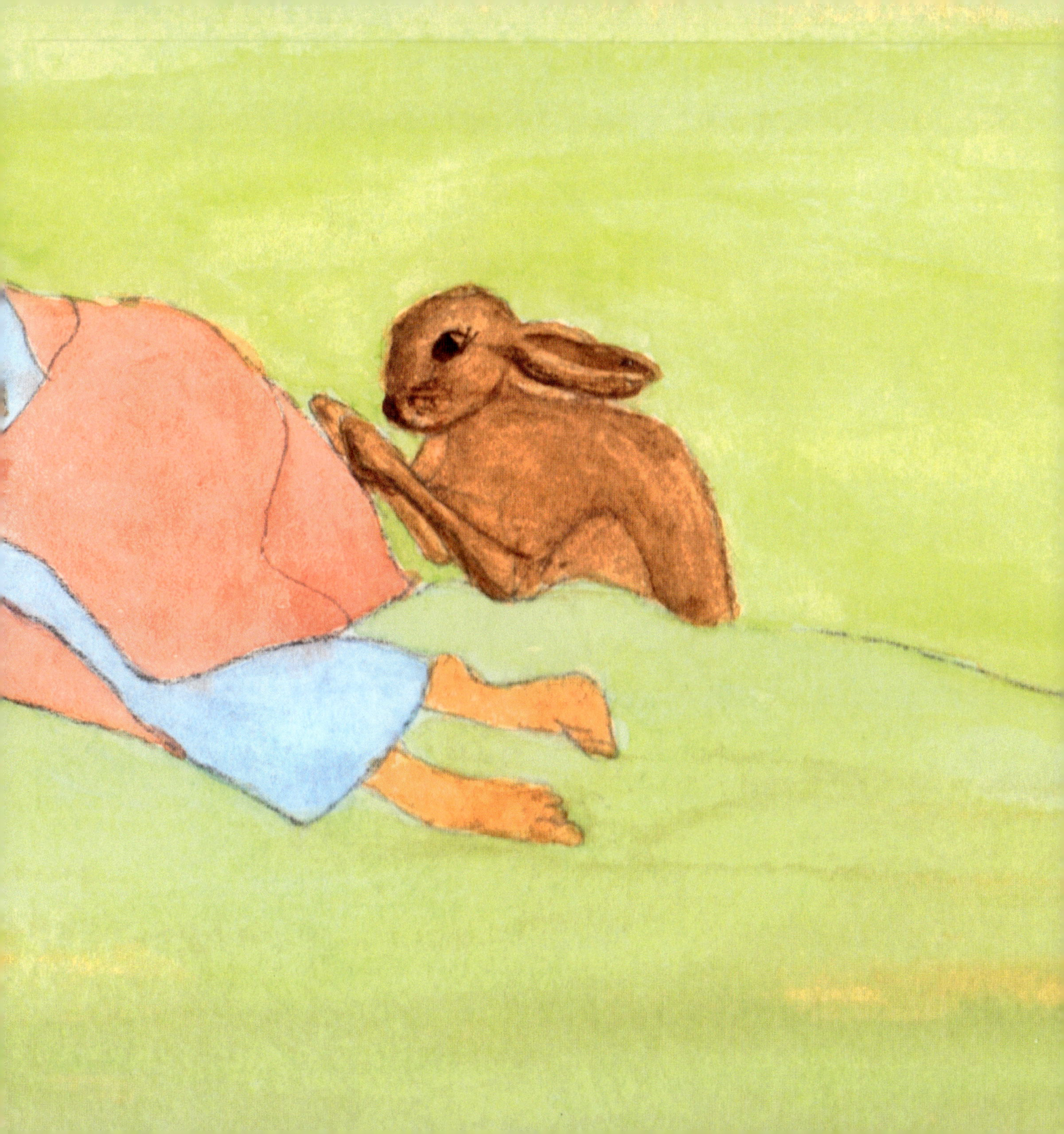

Morning sunlight kissed Easter awake, no man in sight,
Vanished like a whisper in the morning's first light.
He followed distant sounds, a crowd's joyful cheer,
Hoping for a new wonder, he crept near, near.
Through blossoms and branches, he ventured so sly,
Spying a horse-mounted man beneath the blue sky.
But then, a louder cheer drew his ear to the side,
Another miracle, perhaps, a new wonder to bide.

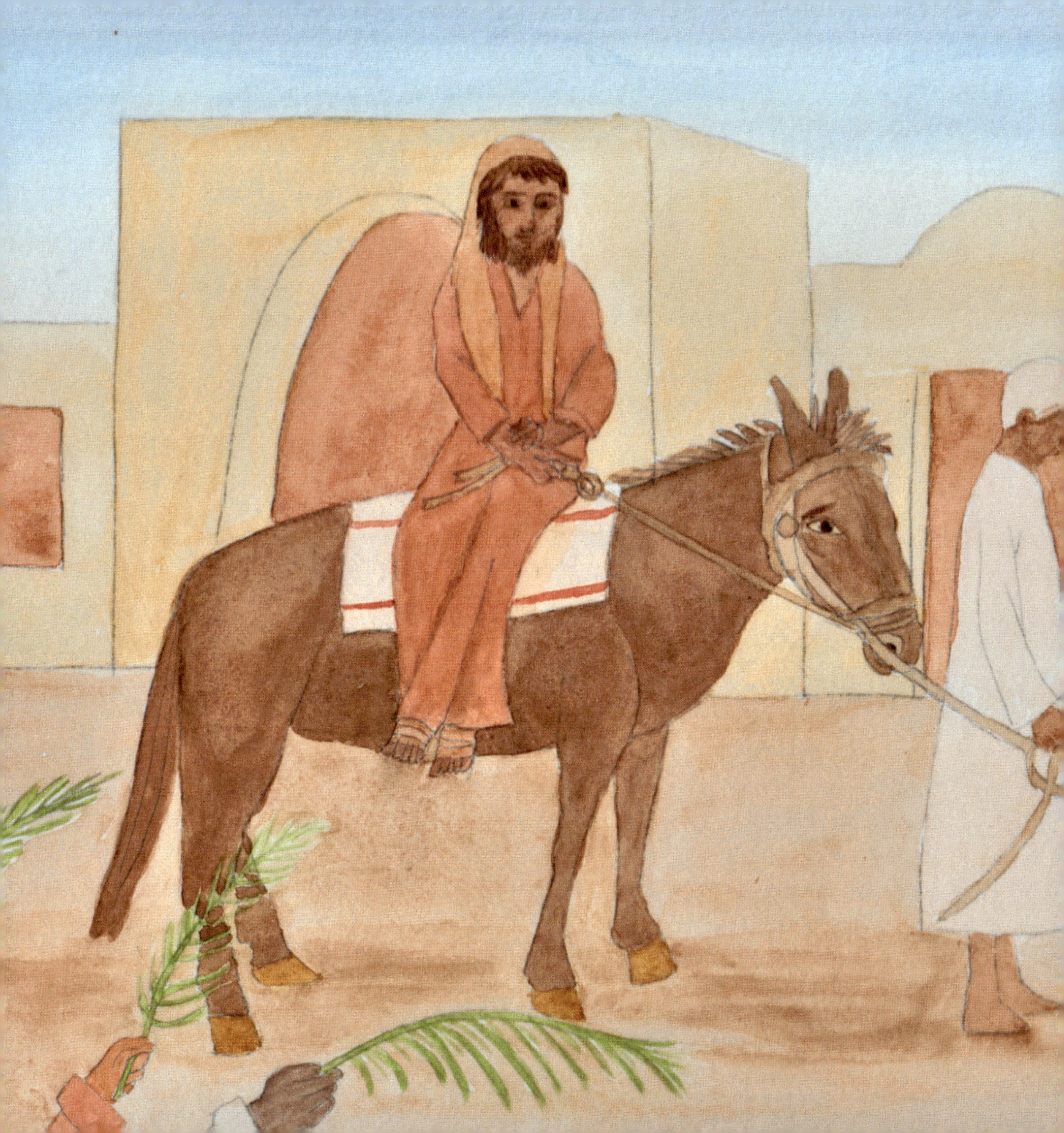

Loud screams and thrown things, what a terrible plight,
Easter startled and panicked, tried to take flight.
A cage closed in, his escape took its toll,
The man on the donkey now so distant, his goal.
Uncertain about clean, but one thing was true,
Easter's yearning for freedom, his heart in a stew.
In the cage, he was fed, a small act of grace,
A boy's secret petting, a brief warm embrace.
But the boy fled in haste when a noise rang so keen,
Reminding dear Easter, he was still "unclean."

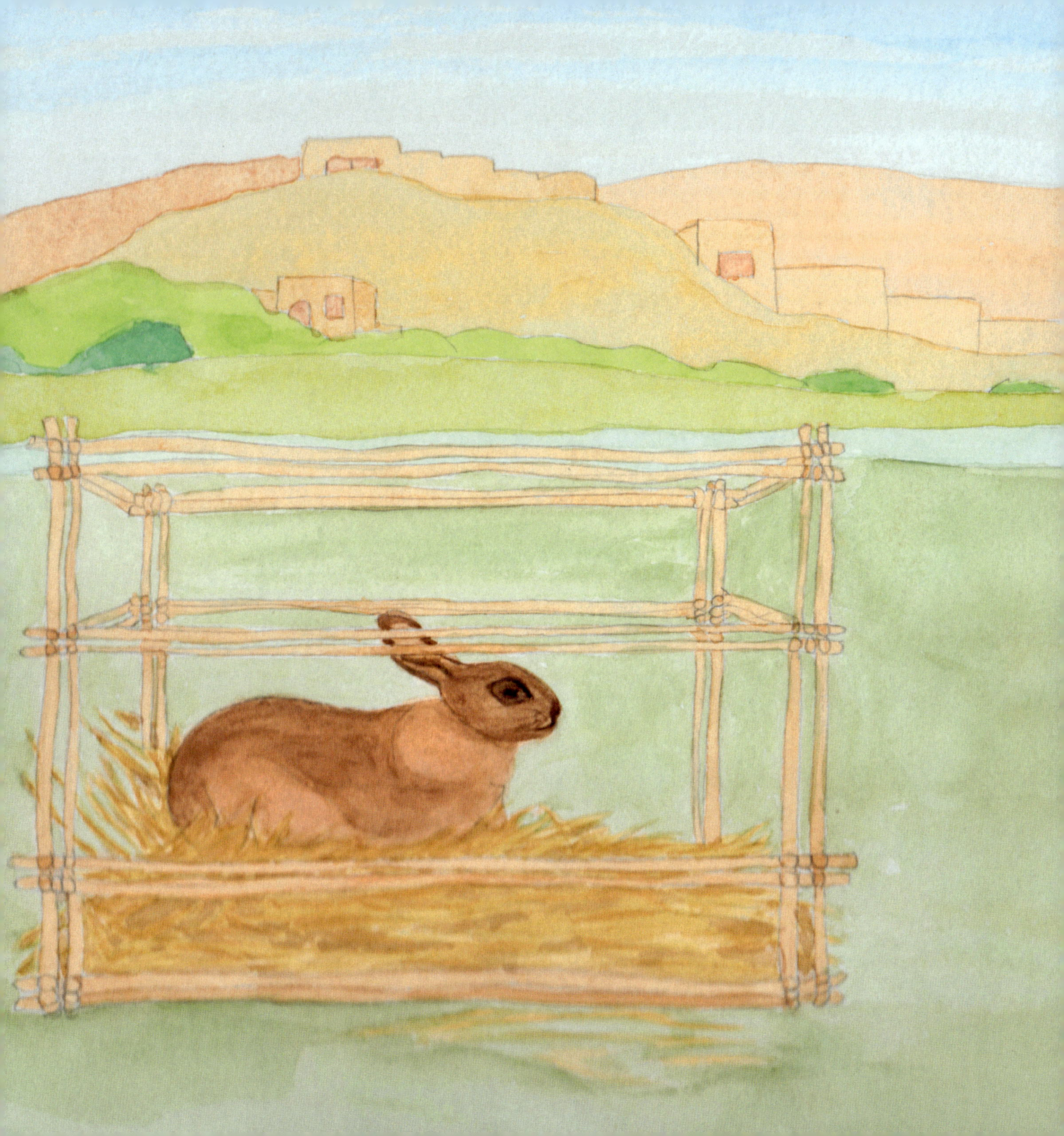

The sun rose on Easter, a bustling display,
People running, commotion, a big day underway.
Amidst the chaos, no heed did they lend,
Our rabbit unnoticed, a furry, lone friend.
And then, just like that, it took but a leap,
The man who'd captured him, in a hurry to sweep.
The cage tumbled over, the door wide ajar,
Freedom at last, oh what a bizarre star!

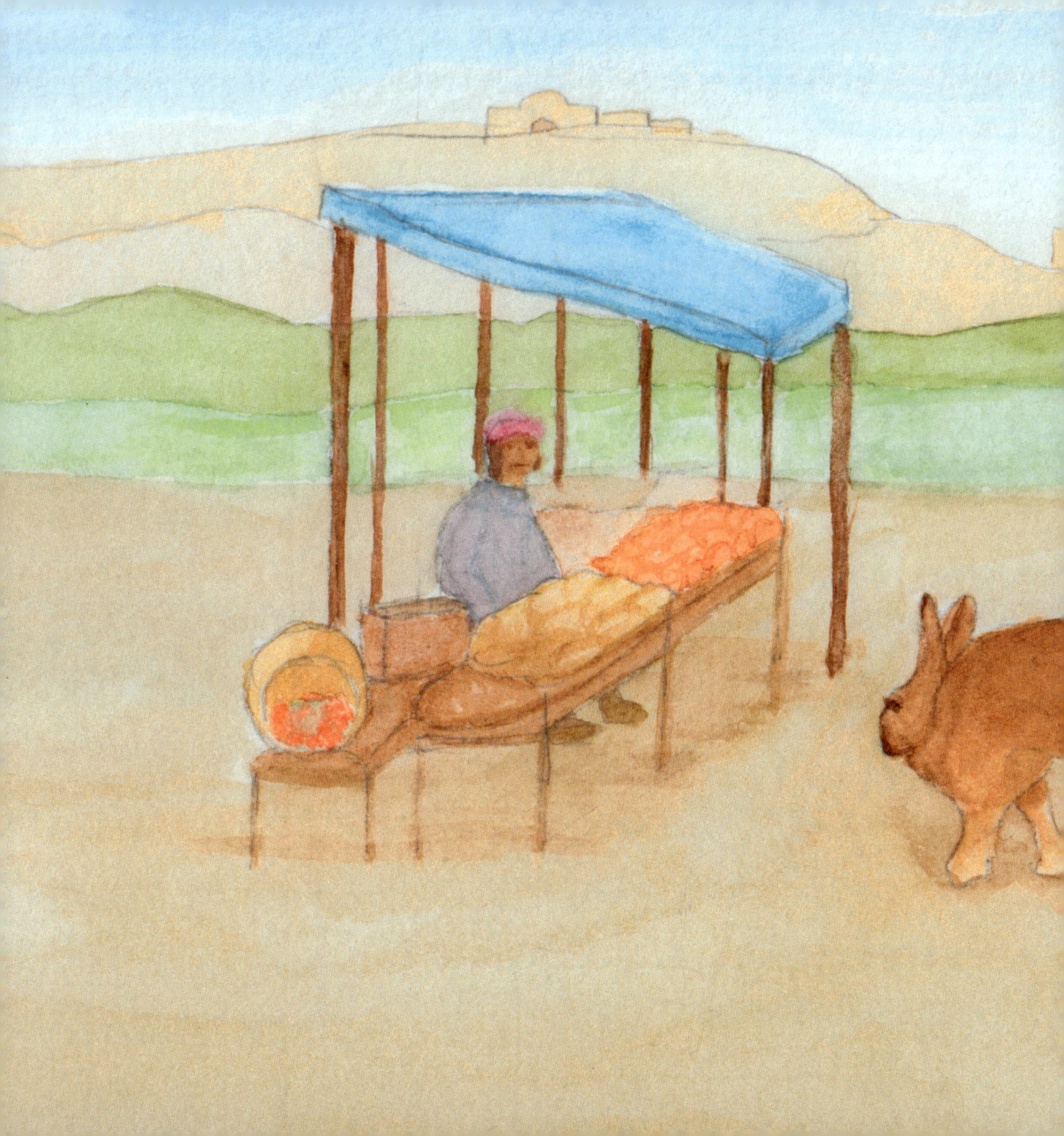

Through the bustling city, he journeyed in stride,
A silent rabbit, he aimed to confide.
But a woman's sharp cry, "Unclean!" pierced the air,
Spooked and alarmed, she knocked powders with flair.
Colours rained down, on eggs painted so bright,
Easter glimpsed their beauty, a quick, wondrous sight.
In a bush, he hid, his heart's frantic beat,
Catching his breath, in leaves' quiet retreat.
Peeked at the world, with a cautious reprieve,
The adventure unfolding, he couldn't believe.

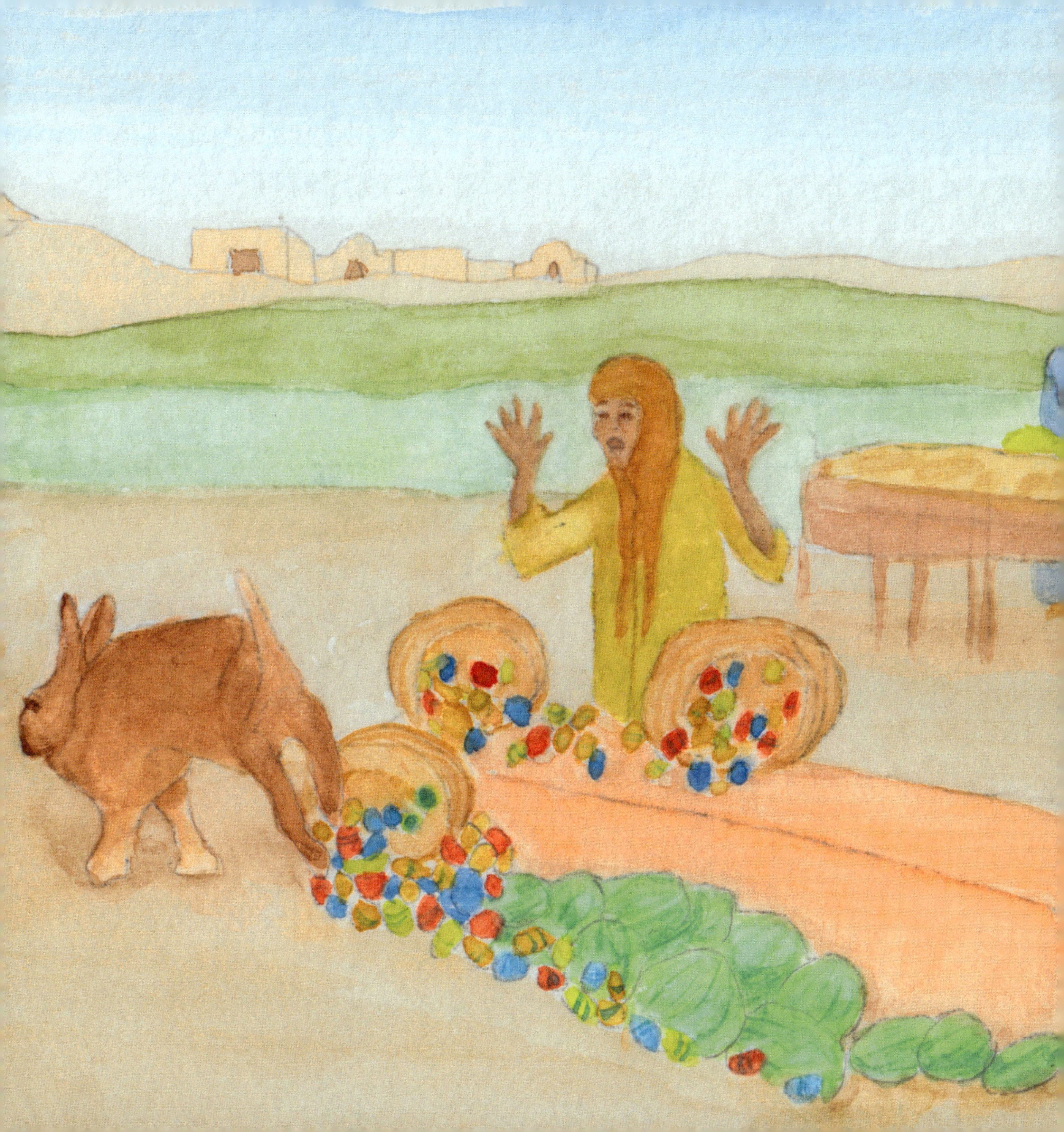

Some folks were laughing, others standing by,
And a few in the distance, just watching the sky.
Easter's gaze fixed upon one weeping soul,
Kneeling by a stake, her tears taking a toll.
He yearned to understand, curiosity spurred,
Hopped closer to see what her heart endured.
Intrigued and concerned, by the stake he did sit,
To discover the reason for her tears, bit by bit.

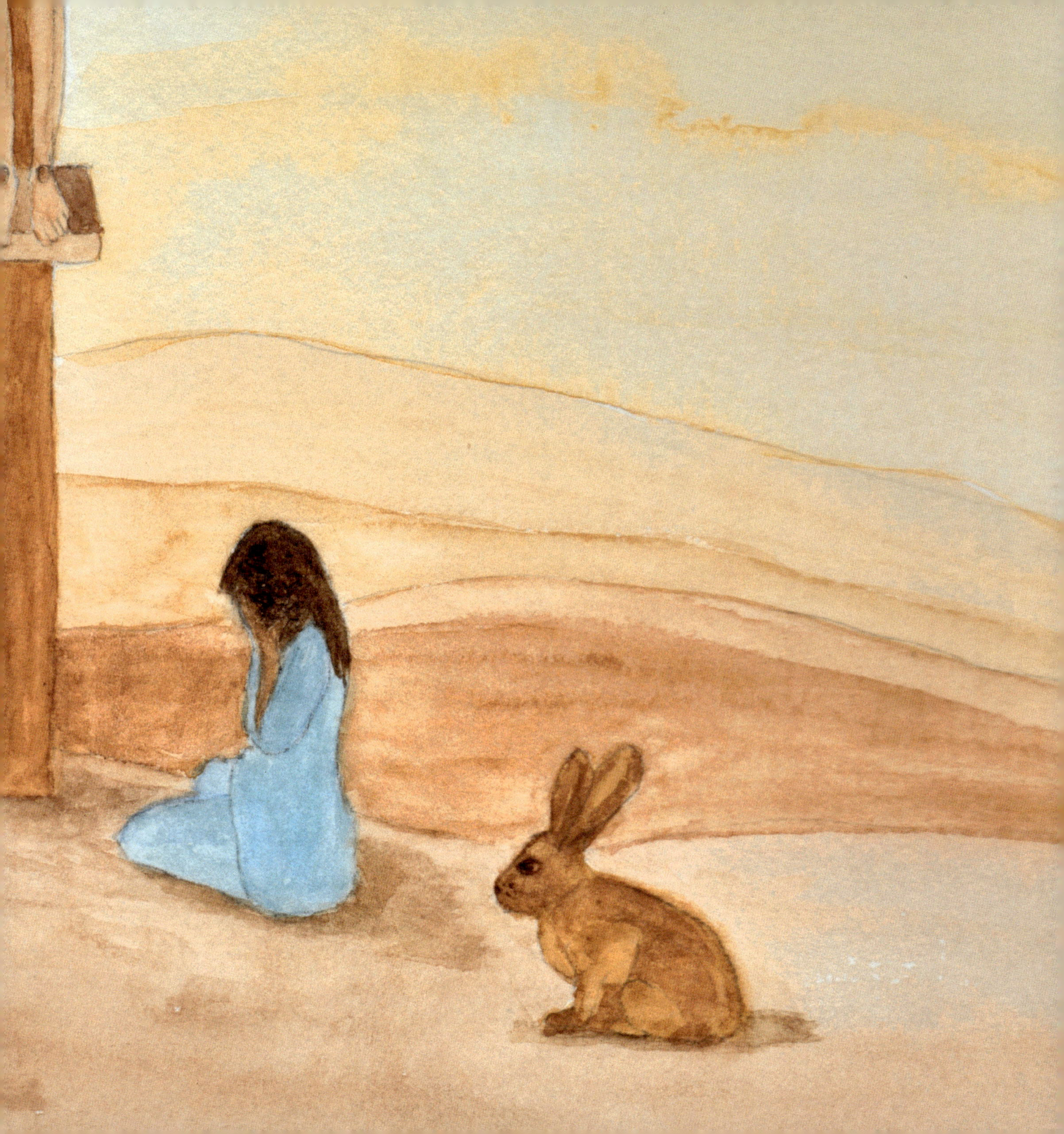

Easter tiptoed closer, eyes wide as a plate,
To witness this scene, to discern his fate.
Aghast and perplexed, as the man he'd discerned,
Hung from the wooden frame, a lesson he'd earned.
The man who'd cleanse him, now silent and still,
A shiver down Easter's spine, a heart-chilling chill.
Uncertainty grew, like a shadow, it loomed,
Would he ever be cleansed? In darkness, he assumed.

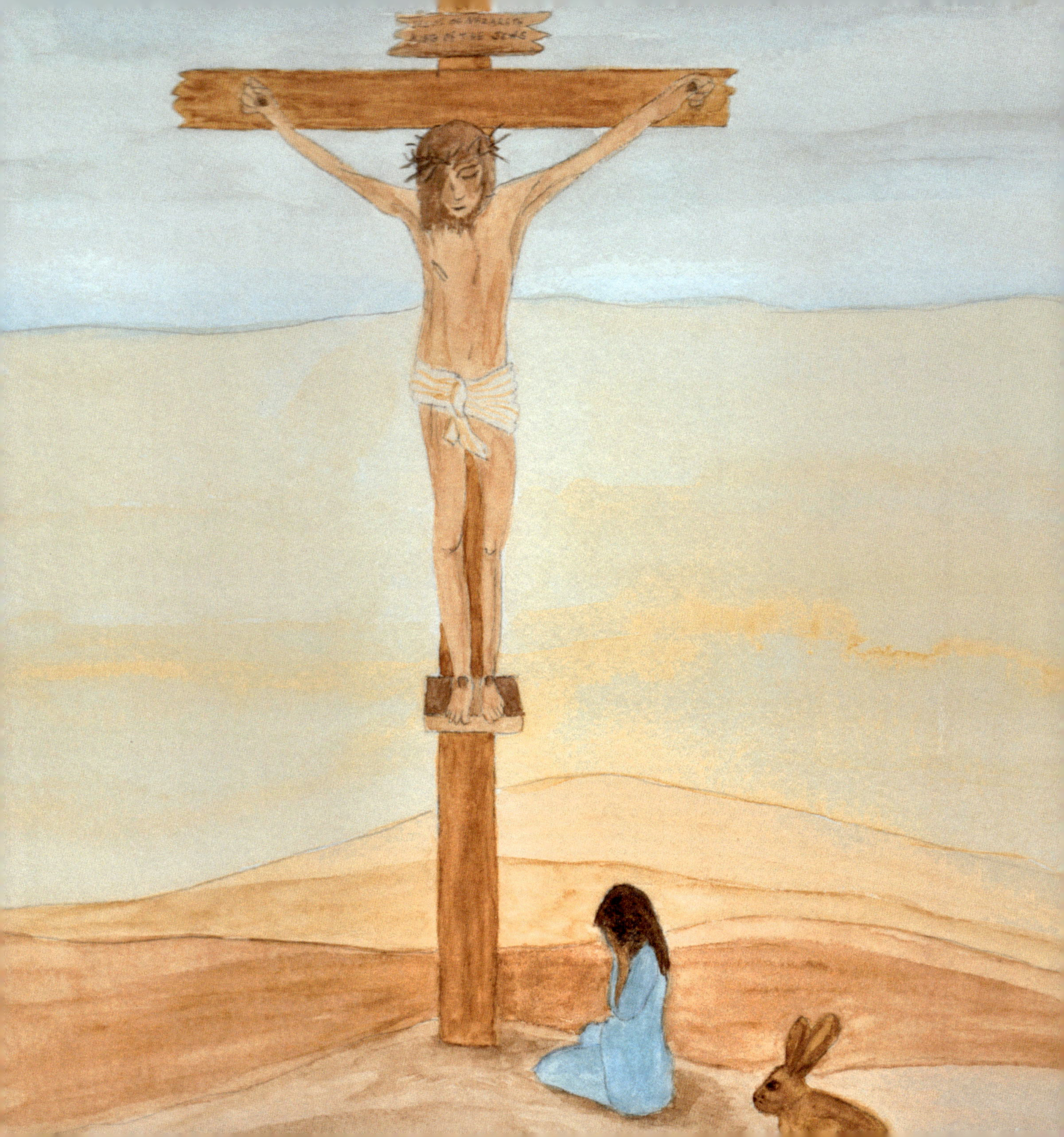

As the man was unhooked, from the wooden display,
Easter made a choice, to follow the woman's way.
Uncertain, like her, on this winding quest's road,
Hoping for answers, their stories to unfold.
From afar, Easter trailed, kept a watchful eye,
As men placed the man in a cave, by and by.
A heavy stone rolled to seal it quite tight,
Mystery unfolding in the fading light.

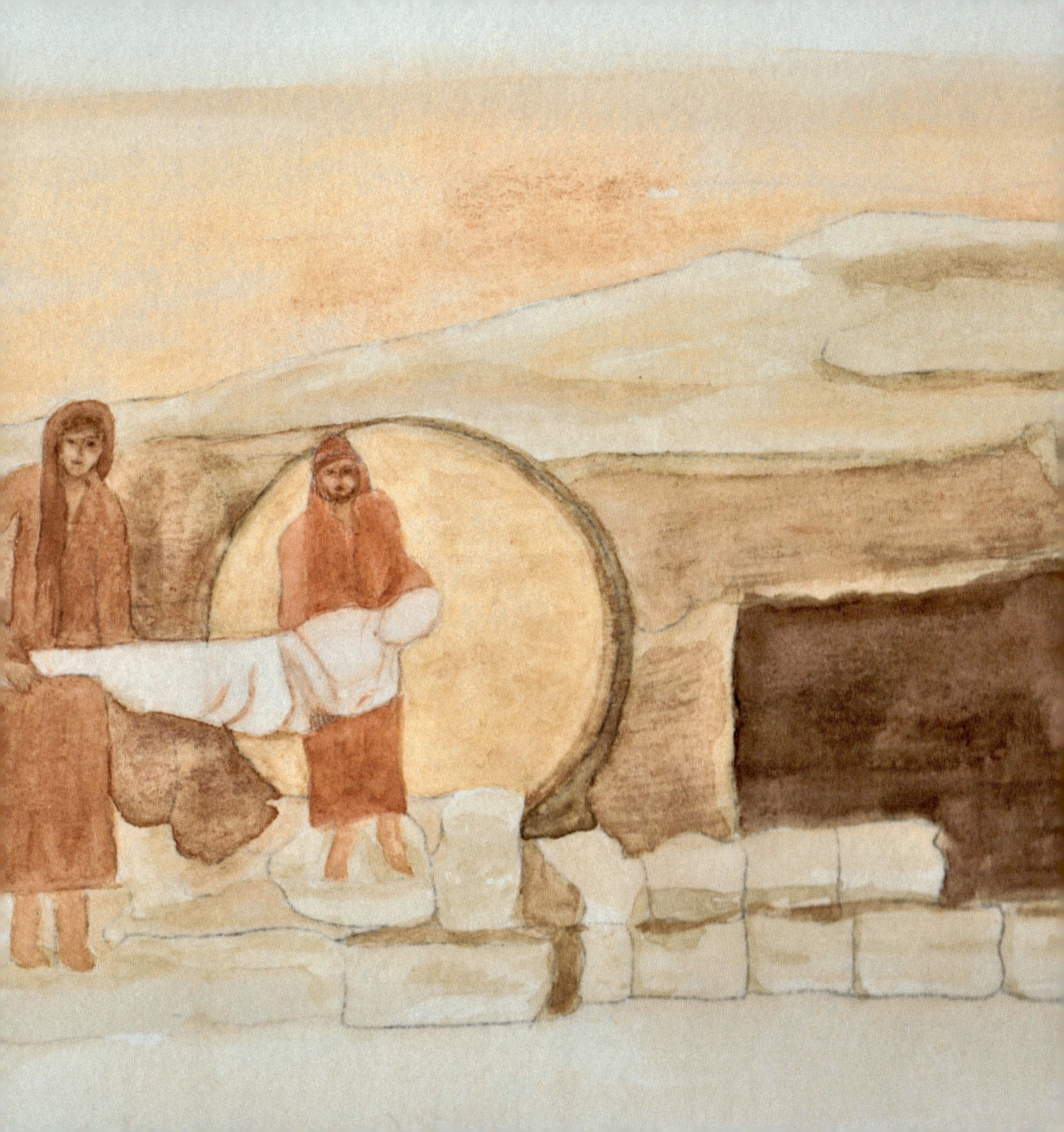

To her house, he followed with steps so light,
But entering her home, he dared not that night.
Outside, he stayed, by a bush so cozy and tight,
Where Easter found rest, in the soft, soothing night.

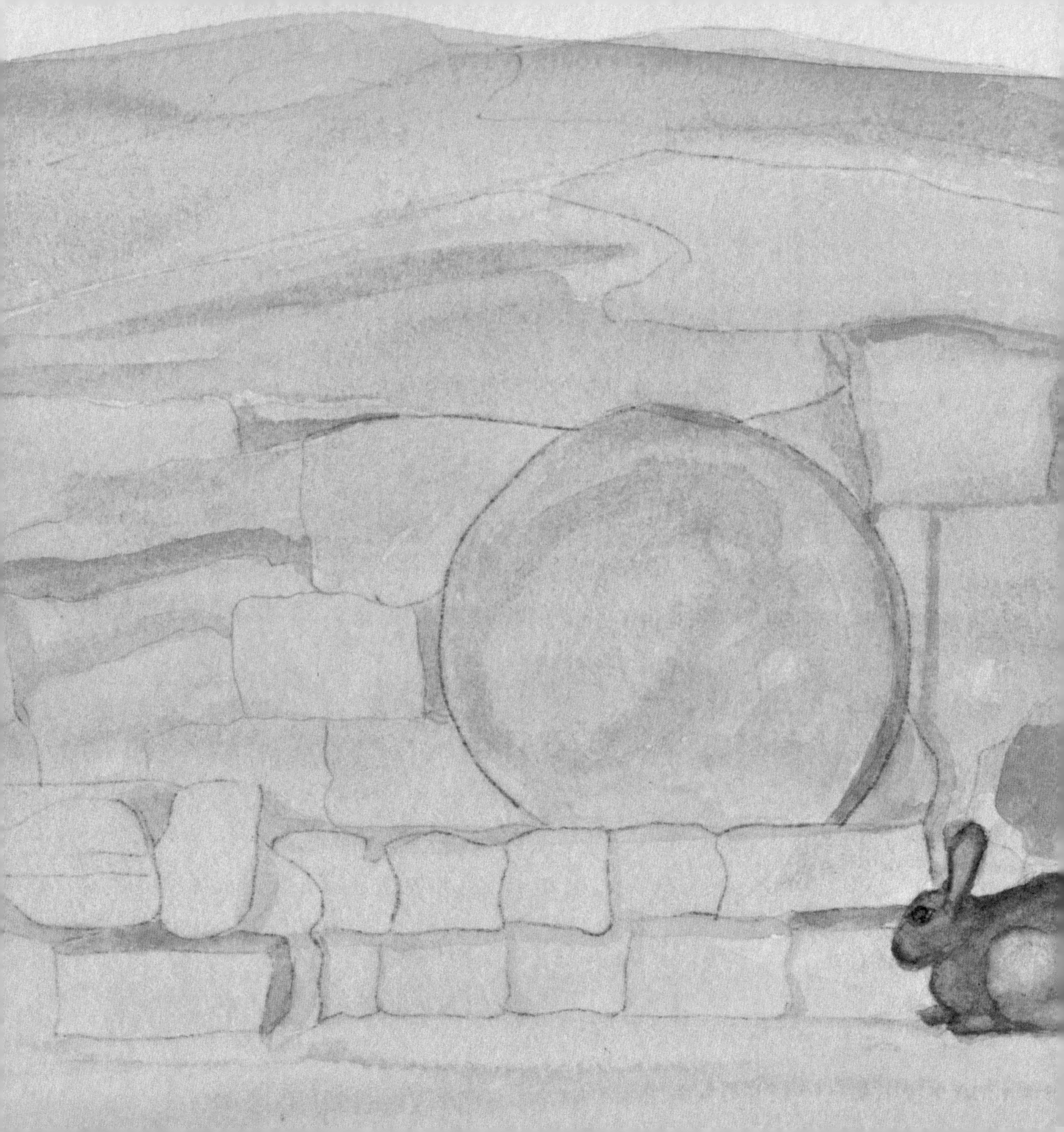

Morning arrived, calm and still,
Occasional cries, a house on a hill.
Easter nestled 'neath the bush, so secure,
Foraging food, feeling safe, reassured.

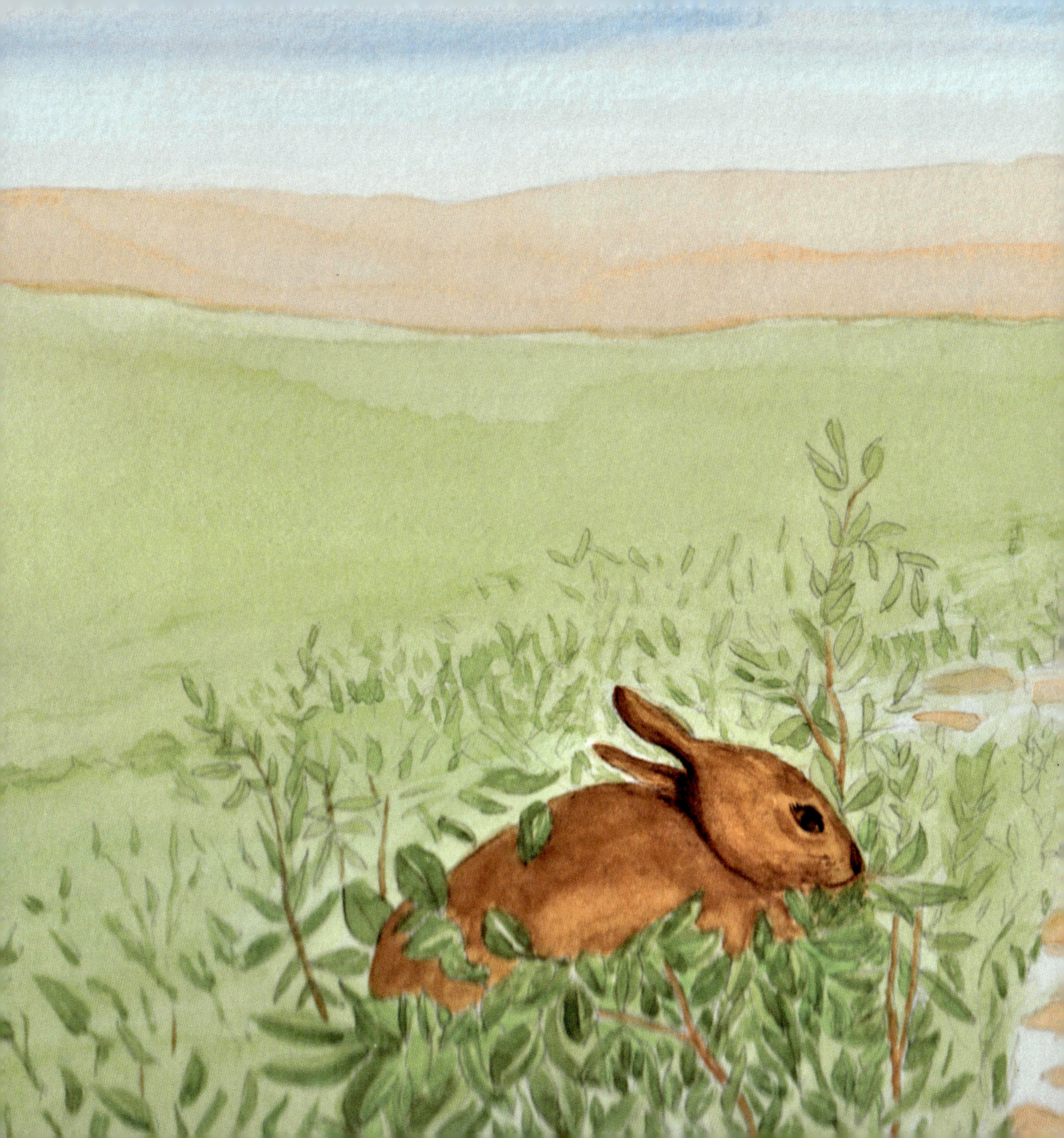

As the sun's early rays began to creep,
Easter awoke from his slumber so deep.
Women chatted, and he took a peep,
Poking his head out of the hole, not making a peep.
Their voices so soft, their steps light as air,
Easter's curiosity, he couldn't help but dare.
Following their path, with a hushed, cautious care,
Towards the cave where the man lay, unaware.

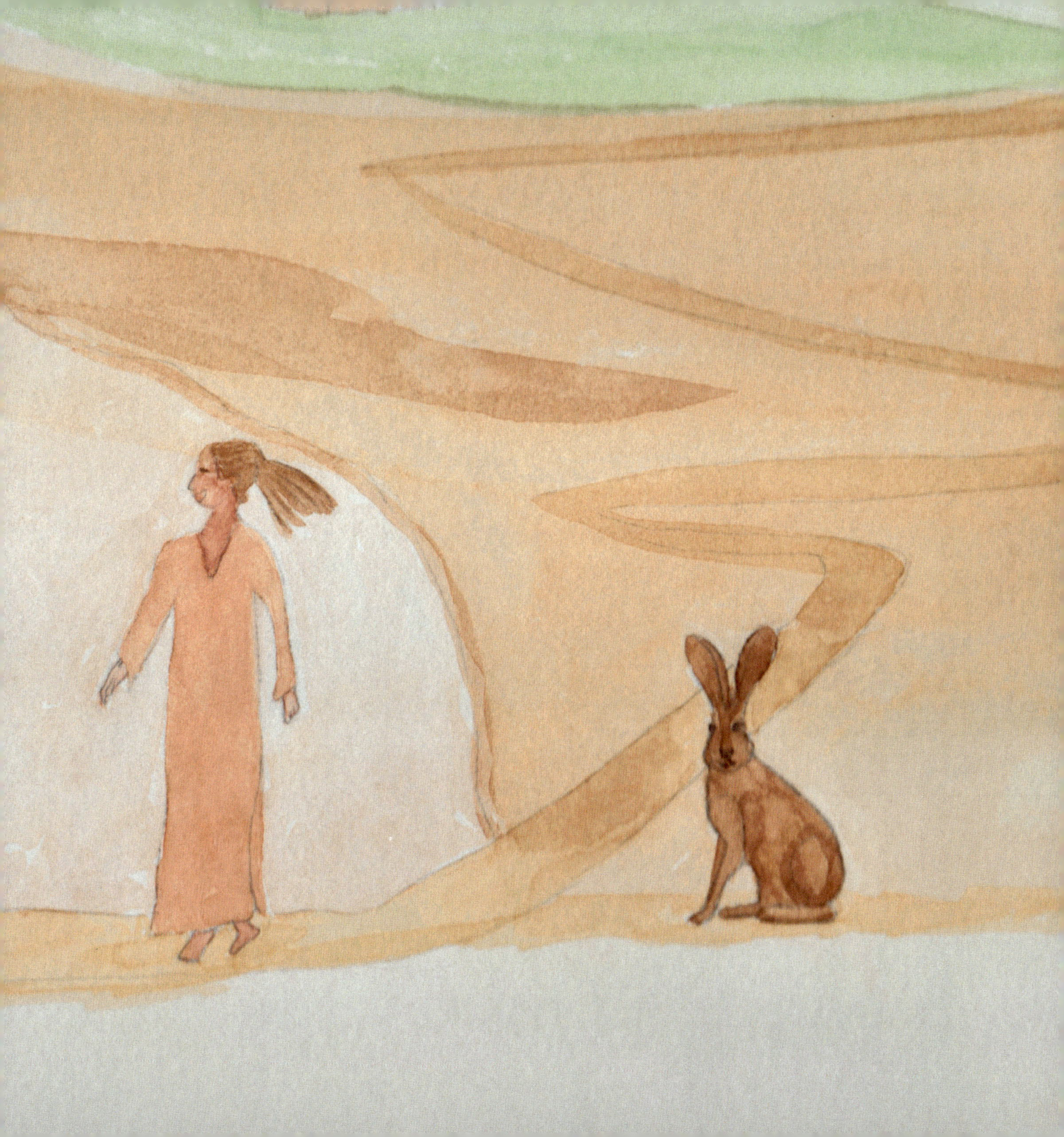

At the cave, the women's excitement took flight,
The stone rolled away, oh, what a sight!
The woman he'd followed sat with tears so bright,
Joy in her heart, as Easter's ears caught the light.
One voice rang out, "He must be alive!" they cheered,
Easter sensed something wondrous had appeared.
Hope filled the air, joy so sincere,
In this moment, something new was near.

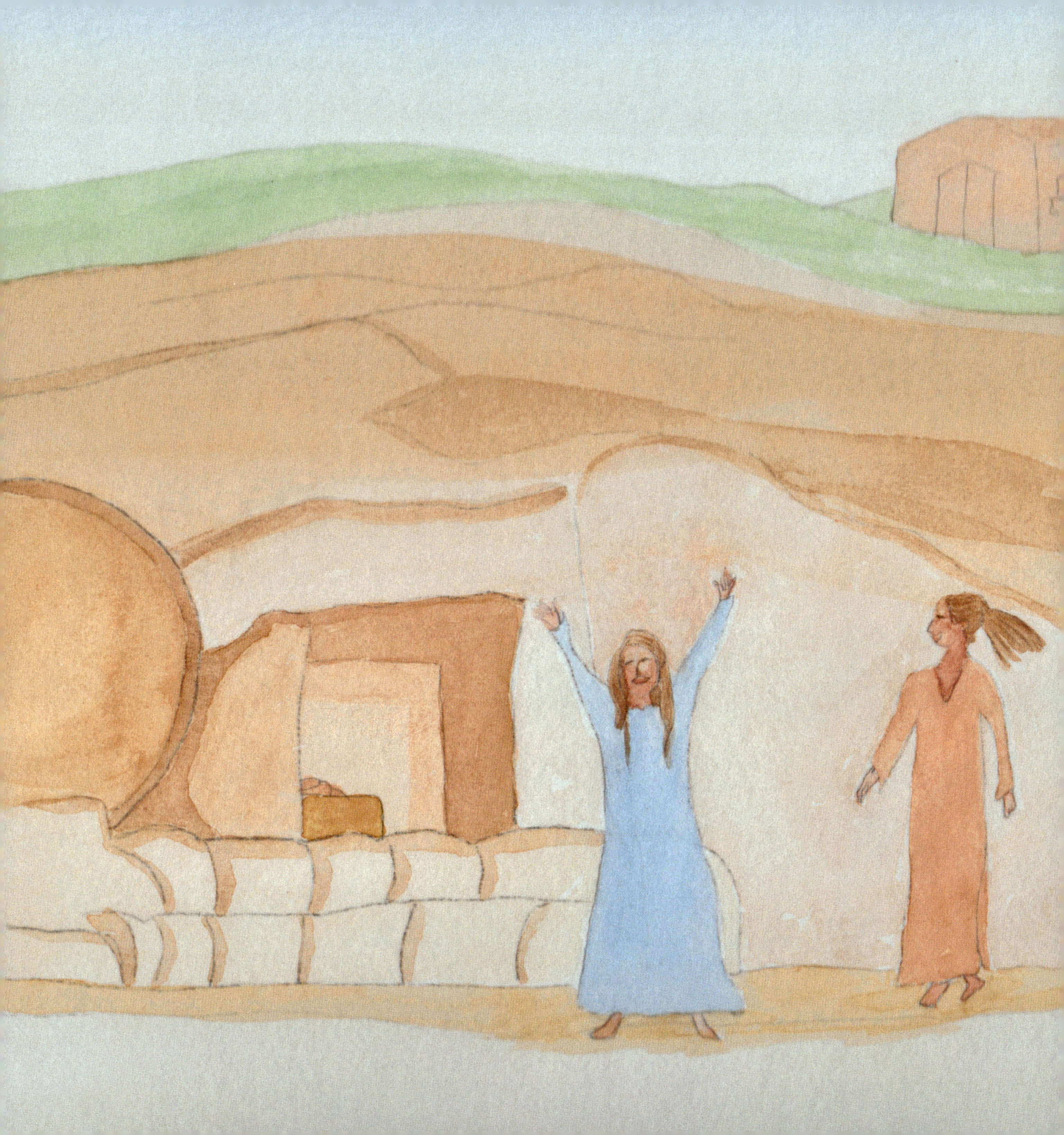

Easter's floppy ears stood in amazement and doubt,
Could it be real, could his hope turn about?
Overwhelmed with joy, he began to move out,
Drawn near to the rock where the woman sat, no doubt.
Easter's heart was gripped by a shiver so deep,
Fear surged in his veins, making his heartbeat leap.
Trembling in stillness, he dared not make a peep,
Worried a cry of "Unclean" would wake from its sleep.

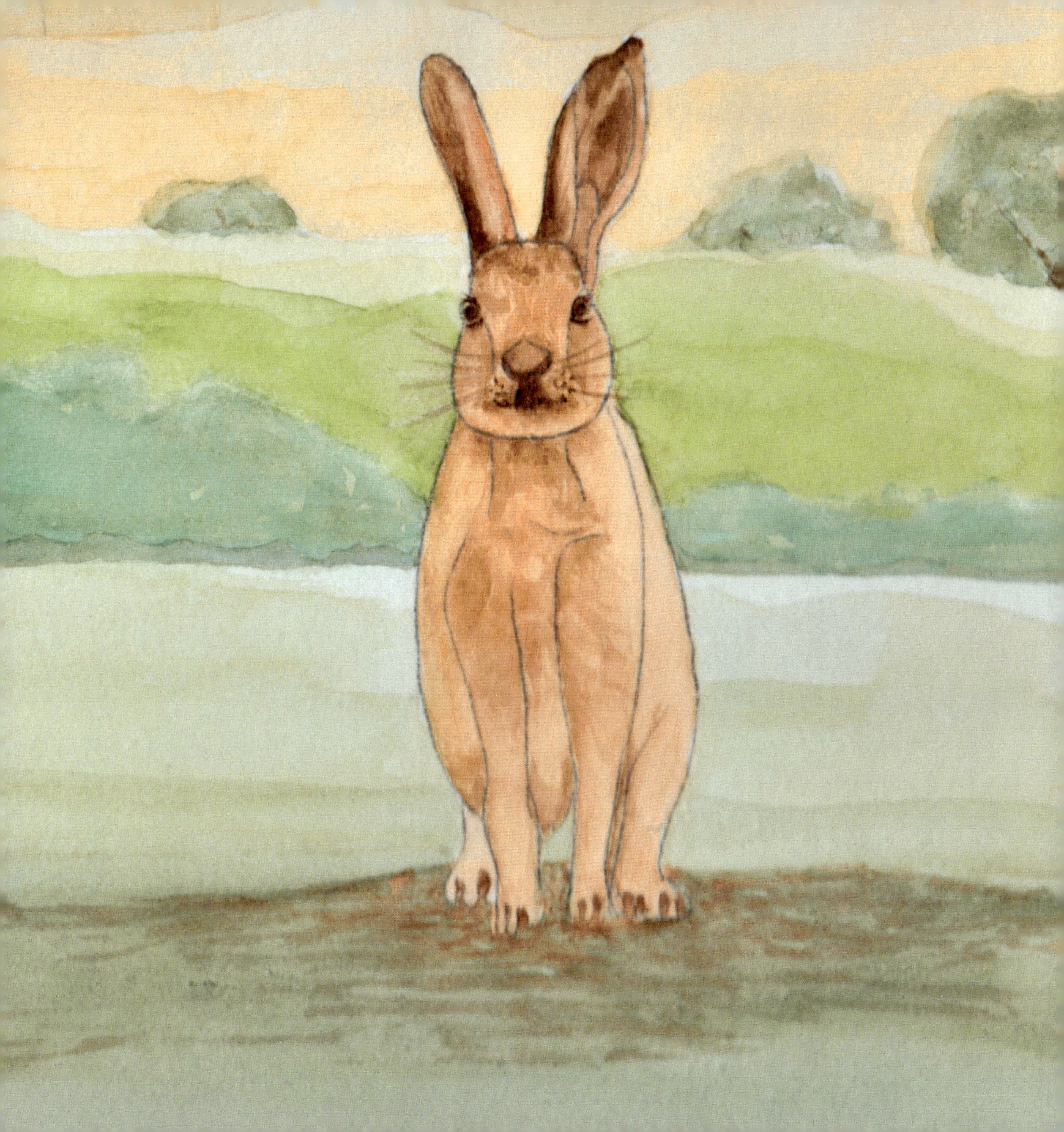

Then, a gentle touch on his fur, like a soothing stream,
Warmth flowed through him, as if in a dream.
Did she not see his "unclean" ream?
Other women might spoil, his heart's precious gleam.
He slowly looked up, met her gaze so sincere,
With tears in her eyes, she whispered in his ear,
"My son has made you clean," her voice crystal clear,
A moment so sacred, Easter held dear.

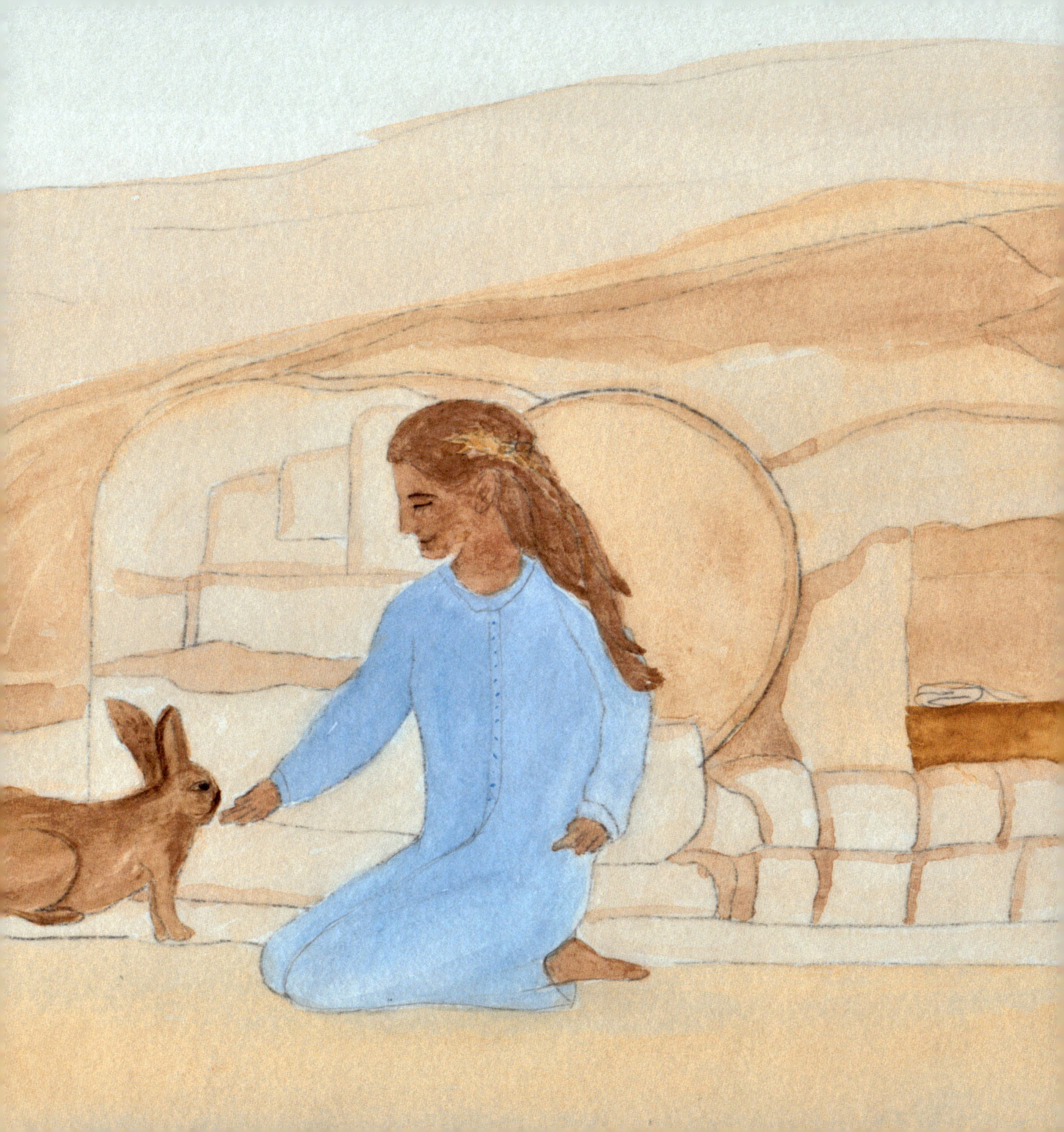

At that moment, Easter the Rabbit transformed, it's true,
Cleansed by Jesus, he and friends anew.
He showed the world what belief could do,
Now rabbits symbolize rebirth, old and new.
Just like Easter the rabbit, you and I may find,
Cleansing in our hearts, in faith entwined.
Believe in the man, in goodness aligned,
Easter's tale of rebirth, for all of humankind.

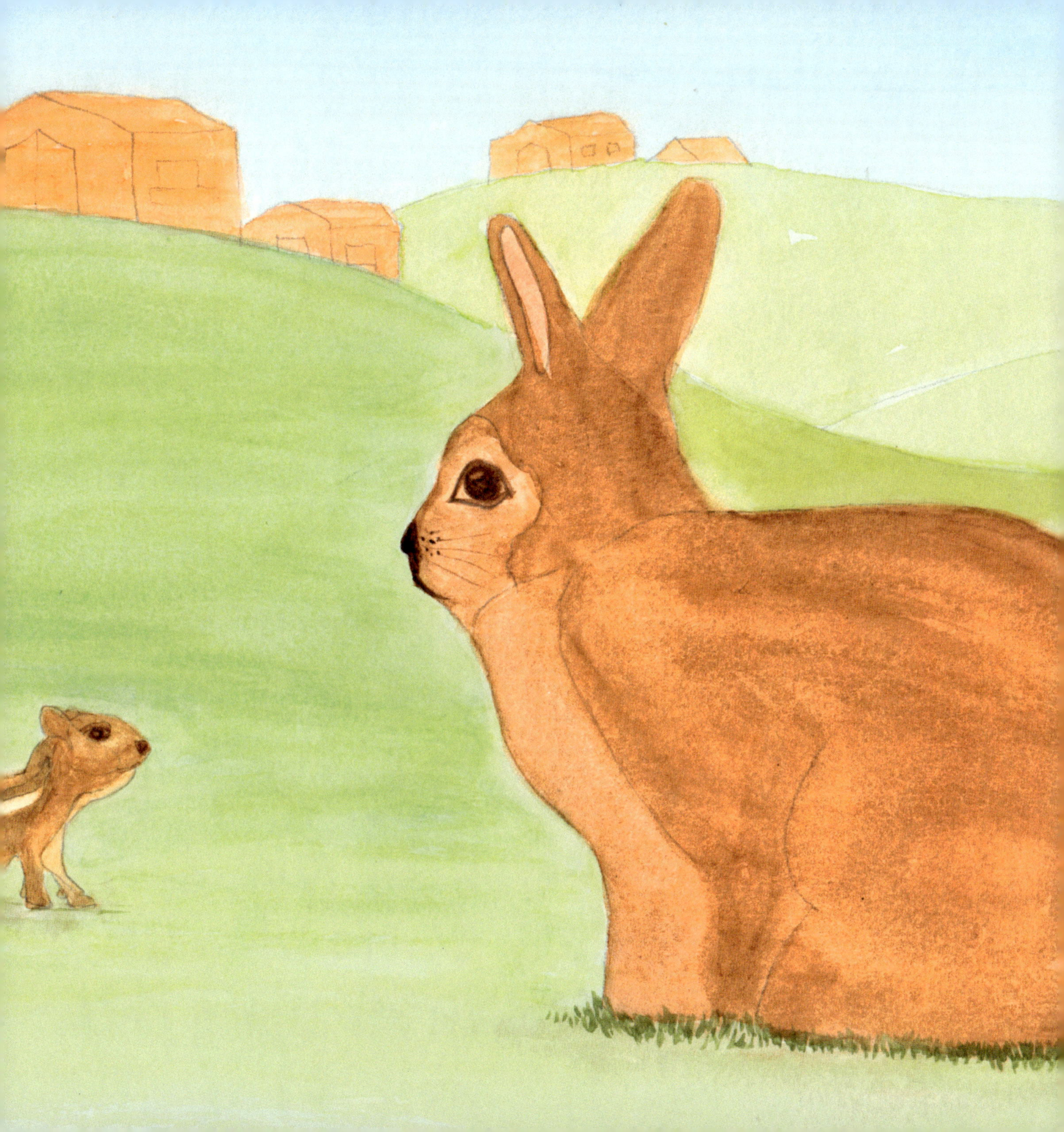

In our story, just as Jesus made Easter the rabbit clean, he can make us clean too. Jesus has a special gift for us, a gift that helps us feel pure and free from our worries and mistakes. All we need to do is believe in Jesus and his love. We can ask for his gift of being clean from sin, and make a promise to follow him. Just like Easter the rabbit found his clean moment, we can find our clean moment with Jesus, feeling light and happy, knowing we are loved just the way we are when we believe in him and follow his loving path.

To start, repeat the prayer written below and find a loving church to help you on your journey.

"Dear Jesus,

Thank you for your love and for making us clean. I want to believe in you and follow your loving path. Please come into my heart and be with me always. Help me to be kind, loving, and make good choices. I want to be your friend and be close to you.

In your name, I pray.

Amen."

Manufactured by Amazon.ca
Bolton, ON